The Irrelevance
and Relevance of
the Christian Message

The Irrelevance
and Relevance of
the Christian Message

Edited by
Durwood Foster

PAUL
TILLICH

Reproduced by permission of
Pilgrim Press

Wipf & Stock
PUBLISHERS
Eugene, Oregon

Wipf and Stock Publishers
199 W 8th Ave, Suite 3
Eugene, OR 97401

The Irrelevance and Relevance of the Christian Message
By Tillich, Paul and Foster, Durwood
Copyright©1996 Pilgrim Press

ISBN 13: 978-1-55635-211-9
ISBN 10: 1-55635-211-5

Publication date 1/23/2007
Previously published by Pilgrim Press, 1996

Contents

Preface

For retrieving Paul Tillich's Earl Lectures from prolonged obscurity, theology and the churches are indebted above all to my distinguished colleague Charles S. McCoy, Professor Emeritus of the Pacific School of Religion. Having orchestrated the lectures in February 1963, Professor McCoy never gave up hope for their publication, although Tillich was unable, during the hectic two and a half years prior to his final illness, to fulfill the agreement to provide a text. All that existed were the audiotapes and a skimpy outline in two handwritten recensions (fourteen and eighteen pages) in the Tillich Archive at Harvard Divinity School. There was an impression among Tillich scholars that the lectures were too inchoate to yield an acceptable book. However, continuing to pursue the matter with Mutie Tillich Farris, when she became her father's literary executor, and with Dr. Richard Brown of Pilgrim Press, Professor McCoy finally got things rolling with a preliminary transcription that showed promise along with textual problems. The largely extempore exposition had been rife with divagations, entanglements, and elusive utterances.

When Dr. Farris and Dr. Brown asked me to establish an absolutely accurate verbatim text and then editorially smooth out that text, I was happy to accept the task, even though quite aware of how opposed Tillich was to the printing of anything of his that did not meet the highest standards. The sense of the verbatim text, which will now be offered to the Tillich archives at Harvard and in Germany, was the uppermost criterion in preparing the edited version presented here. Readability was also a continuous consideration. Punctuation was introduced in keeping with the oral rhythm, but with shortening of sentences where feasible. Some paragraphs, where Tillich's asides had scrambled the implicit order, were restructured, but always with an effort to retain flavor and his remarkable sense of the audience. Very occasionally words were substituted where Tillich had used a misleading German cognate instead of the English obviously intended. The lecture hall setting was gently transposed to that of a book, and gender was inclusivized, as Tillich would surely have wanted in a current publication.

Finally, besides heartily thanking Dr. McCoy on behalf of all concerned, I am immensely grateful to Dr. Carol Voisin for painstaking help in getting the verbatim text exactly right, and to Sarah Lewis, M.A., M.A.S., for her unstinting assistance in decisions about wording in the edited text, as well as in proofreading. Professor Sharon Burch of Boston University deserves thanks for serving as liaison with the Harvard Tillich Archive, as do Dr. Farris and Dr. Brown for their friendly, patient encouragement at every stage.

Durwood Foster

Introduction

I

Paul Tillich's 1963 Earl Lectures give a surprising new look after all these years, not only at one of the century's theological giants, but at the situation of the churches then and now, as we ponder Christianity's relevance to the contemporary world. Much of the vast sweep of Tillich is spontaneously summed up here, as only he could have done it, speaking from sparse notes, personably and candidly, to both poles of his life's calling as theologian of culture *and* interpreter of the Christian message. We have in these lectures, as nowhere else with such brevity, the fully rounded out Tillich. The monumental *Systematic Theology* has just been completed, Germany, Union, and Harvard are behind him, and Chicago, Santa Barbara, and world travel now whet for the very last phase his unflagging dialogic zeal. He mounts the podium here as indisputably the most extolled and also the most questioned theologian in North America, if not the world. An overflow audience, incipiently aware of seismic religious rumblings, waits with bated breath. Fundamentalists as well as radicals picket outside—after all, this is Berkeley—and Tillich knows half his hearers are pastors while others are university intellectuals, divinity scholars, and spiritual mavericks in every state of doubt. In a poignantly tight three hours he has to remobilize his whole venerable career of "mediating" between modernity and the Gospel. Happily, Pacific School of Religion has not prescribed a topic. He has complete leeway, as he almost never had when his mind and heart were most mature, to state for such a public his own most pressing concerns.

II

From the beginning nothing was more characteristic of Tillich than what he called the "method of correlation." He relentlessly insisted that authentic theology—and all the more so authentic preaching—must speak to the burning issues of human life. The failure of conventional "God-talk" to take those issues seriously provoked his quip that nowadays, "To be a theologian one has to be a non-theologian," as that might be pursued with "secular" literature, art, and philosophy. Yet for Tillich inescapably, nurtured as he was in the bosom of the church, attention to the human condition was only half the battle. For the other half he categorically affirmed, in principle, Karl Barth's valiant attempt to hold Christian witness accountable to the biblical Word. In spite of their sometimes strident discords, Tillich consistently admired Barth as the champion of message-centered (kerygmatic) theology, and saw his own main responsibility as "answering theology" which would open up the relevance of the message to its intended recipients. Nevertheless, for this labor itself there were always two sides to the theological street. Along with the rigorous analysis of the "human question," searched out in all realms of culture and society, there was the corresponding urgency to discern afresh how "the New Being in Jesus as the Christ," as Tillich named the saving power of the Gospel, may best be formulated to free and heal sin-wracked humanity. For anyone who reads them, the Earl Lectures will surely quash the notion that Tillich was only a religious philosopher not interested in the church. On the contrary, it takes involvement to chide the church as severely as he does here, for its obtuseness and political correctness, its legalism and brainwashed retreat to mere spirituality. Tillich's strictures unmistakably issue from distressed passion.

The human situation which is one pole of the method of correlation is, of course, continually changing in its social and cultural configuration. For Tillich this was axiomatic, as it was for so many others who, like him, were heirs of Troeltsch. Therefore the theological task is never finished but is always posed again somewhat differently by the incessant dynamism of history. Tillich's singular gift for depicting the shifts of the historical context led to notable publications throughout his career, culminating in the *Systematic Theology*, where each of the five major parts renews analysis of the human problem from the aspect of the "revelatory answer" under scrutiny in that part. Challenged, as he often was, regarding the finality of *his* reading of the human problem, he emphasized that no theology—certainly including his own—is the last word in rendering either the question or the answer. He always urged, as he does in these lectures, that anyone with better information or different questions should bring them to the fore. Thus the priority of responsible correlation intrinsically outranked for Tillich the status of his own analysis. We follow him best when we stay "wide open" (a phrase he liked) for the reality of *our* time and place.

The upheavals in theology that were about to occur under the several banners of "liberation" were not foreseen by Tillich any more than by others. Yet few if any Christian thinkers had done more than he to prepare for the erupting indictments of economic oppression, sexism, and racism. Had he been able to keep his appointment with the New School for Social Research to return to New York in the fall of 1965—instead of dying that October—doubtless his critique and encouragement would have thickened the plot of all the new movements. Much of his early initiative had flowed into religious socialism—one of the things that earned him the enmity of the Nazis—and a sense for Realpolitik registers steadily in his subsequent utterances, including the lectures before us. When the gender consciousness of Simone de Beauvoir began to stir Union Seminary in the early 1950s, it was Tillich again that alert women students first turned to, and his struggle against masculine one-sidedness in the basic Christian symbols (of the Trinity, for instance) clearly influenced feminist/womanist thought. Moreover, while there is no way to excuse the theological establishment as a whole for compliance with institutional racism, Tillich not only consistently aroused "questioning from below," but linked *power* with justice and love over against the dehumanizing management of persons. It is of a piece with all this that Tillich's personal comportment was affirmed by so many of both genders and all races as memorably liberating.

Two other theological storm fronts that graphically marked the situation of the 1960s were the "death of God" and the "theology of hope." These also may appear to be missing from Tillich's purview, and he did not in fact anticipate either their idiom or their vitality. Yet it was generally recognized at the time that the debunking of the "God up there"—the God the first sputnik reported *not* sighting—was a (rather irresponsible) popularization of Tillich's long-standing critique of an objectified deity who is simply *a* being above others. The Earl format—180 minutes in toto—permitted only the barest pointers to the nuanced parsing of the *Systematic Theology,* but the lectures still show how thoroughly alert Tillich was to radical secularism (what he preferred to call "profanization"), the content of the death of God. They also show that he viewed this situation as not only partly true—as de facto our cultural condition—but more deeply as the problem itself: the lostness of the dimension of the vertical, that is, religious transcendence. As for the "theology of hope," Tillich had retrieved effectively in the third volume of his magnum opus what is palpable in his early work but less evident in the first two volumes of the systematics: an exposition of the Kingdom of God as within history as well as eschatological. Moreover, his vision of the Kingdom is explicitly social and political, not merely personal. This theme of hope was also expressed by Tillich in terms of finitude's "essentialization," the fruition throughout history of the potential of everything created. Tillich took sin extremely seriously, but the fruition of creation still goes forward irrepressibly as salvation from sin. So he was profoundly hopeful. However, he could readily be seen as *not hopeful enough,* if one espoused a form of utopianism. Here Tillich would have spoken critically to some versions of the theology of hope as well as some representations of feminist and ethnic liberation. While prophetic in judging the status quo, utopianism, for him, was too unwary of sin and too optimistic about finitude itself, thereby ignoring the eternity of the Kingdom. He would have perceived the debacle of communism as a case in point, showing the vacuum of despair in the wake of disillusionment. Still, he abjured resignation even more than utopianism and, as these lectures show, continued to seek transformation courageously. If once, in pre-Hitler times, he had summoned theology forward with drum and fife, even now, after sobering decades, he calls upon us all "to fight an uphill battle" to turn things around ecclesially and culturally.

Far from being obliviously distant from the erupting trends of the sixties, Tillich was thus profoundly interconnected and critically interactive with their rootage and their import. However, in his compressed diagnosis for the Berkeley audience of the irrelevance of contemporary Christian preaching, he dives far beneath the headlines of the decade. He goes for the jugular of Christianity's current malaise within the whole development of modernity. To appreciate the magnitude of his analysis, we have to compare it with that of such towering philosophical peers as Buber, Jaspers, and Heidegger. It is this line of thought that Tillich styles existentialist. As he stresses, the word refers to much more than philosophy. It finds expression in all forms of art, and in life itself, above all as *protest against the dehumanization of the human*. This dehumanization has come about, existentialism tells us—and Tillich drives this home—through the fateful, accelerating ascendancy of *technology*. Technology is the practical enactment of calculating or controlling (= objectified scientific) knowledge. When such knowledge breaks loose from holistic knowledge—when science becomes scientism—it runs amok, insatiably endeavoring to measure and manage. Persons too become the quantified objects of technical control. It is this cultural-industrial octopus of desacralization and dehumanization that Tillich sees as the root of Christianity's widely experienced irrelevance in our time. Racism, sexism, and economic exploitation fatten upon it, as they share with it the taproots of pride, greed, and faithlessness that primordially manifest our fallenness. Today how would Tillich assess cybernetics? The computer has obviously become the flagship tool of controlling knowledge. But must it serve only dehumanization? Here we need to note carefully that what is arraigned in these lectures is a technology unleashed by scientism, ruthlessly unmindful of the humane. A technology devoted to enhancing the humane would be something else again. *Systematic Theology III* lets us glimpse such a technology, ambiguously mingled with the voracious kind. But the positive side of the technological is not developed in the work before us.

Tillich always perceives dialectically. When he sizes up our culture, a one-dimensional survey of megatrends will not do. The human situation he speaks to was in the throes of *both* dehumanizing scientism *and* the existentialist counterculture. The latter went on to become more complex than was often recognized. Yet Tillich, who had imbibed it from the outset, continued to be thought of in terms of the initial phase, when anxiety and the shock of nonbeing were focal. Along with such themes it is generally accepted that he took, notably from Heidegger, the question of Being as crucial for understanding God. For that reason his approach could seem antithetical to Buber's "I-Thou" slant, and the first volume of the *Systematic Theology* supports such a reading. However, the Earl Lectures, if we take them seriously, show how static this conventional picture of Tillich is—how inconsistent it is with the climactic parts of the systematics as well as in occasional statements of the late fifties and the sixties. Just as Jaspers went on to warn of the "sclerosis of objectivity," and the later Heidegger developed his disconcerting reflections on technology—in which he vividly portrayed what our lectures dub "forwardism" (the unappeasable advance of technocracy), so Tillich by no means rested with insights already achieved. Spurred by debate with Buddhist sage Hisamatsu Shin-ichi and by the incisive arguments of process philosophy, creative reconception went on apace in the Tillichian brain. This was demanded and facilitated, of course, by honorific obligations like the Gifford Lectures, the heady challenges of Harvard and Chicago, the reentries into Germany, the visits to Greece, Israel, and Japan, and the restless, hungry audiences he rushed hither and yon to engage. The Earl Lectures are valuable for closely gathering up so much of the grist and spirit of this still evolving Tillich, and for reminding us he has yet to be adequately compared with the postwar existentialists and their successors like Foucault and Derrida, or for that matter with thinkers like Polanyi, Wittgenstein, and Huston Smith. Friction with technology and scientism binds these figures illuminatingly together, confirming that even though labels go out of vogue, Tillich's broad diagnosis still applies.

Besides the profanizing influence of scientism and the swarm of ills it aggravates, there is another challenge to traditional Christianity that has become increasingly acute in our century. This is the rebounding vitality and expansion of the other religions. More than any other of the towering

Christian systematicians who were his peers, Tillich was always mindful of the implicit impeachment of the universality and finality of Christianity by competing world faiths such as Buddhism and Islam and some forms of Hinduism. One of the principal ways he spoke to the matter was to clarify, as Barth also did, that the Christian claim pertains to Christ as norm, and not to Christendom or the churches in their glaring ambiguity. Nevertheless, the problem intensified as the "global village" prophesied by Marshall McLuhan became more and more palpable. The new religious movements also became a factor, as did an invigorated Judaism, and this has been more true since Tillich's death. What about the claims of other religious *norms* over against the Christ norm? This challenge is very far from being resolved, and it is another welcome feature of these Earl Lectures that they are alert to the burgeoning encounter with other religions, especially Buddhism. As the team-teaching with Mircea Eliade shows, and indeed the final address in Chicago, this encounter was for the late Tillich a foremost agenda item. Toward the end he said with pathos that, if he could start over on his *Systematic Theology,* he would write it with much greater appreciation of world religions.

III

Though his views were always under fire from both the theological right and the left, in his lifetime Tillich was recognized by many as an eminent inquirer into the human question, and also as a powerful witness to the Christian answer. It is remarkable how masterfully he fulfilled both functions, sometimes leaning in more to the one and sometimes more to the other. In Dresden and Frankfurt early on, and then late, when called to Harvard as university professor, he scintillated as a philosopher of culture. Through the middle decades, on the other hand, he was a teacher of preachers, albeit in "philosophical" theology. His steadfastly pursued "great work" was a systematic theology, while his sermons were hailed by many as his best teaching. Truly he was a bridge figure whose versatile expertise was hard to show on a single map. It may still surprise some that the Earl Lectures, venting what is "most on his heart and conscience," focus as they do on the church and preaching. It is surely a valuable feature that they evince Tillich's ecclesial loyalty in unabashed union with his philosophical proclivities. Moreover, they reveal the weathered veteran winnowing out what for him, in his seventy-sixth year, is tried and true—the core Christian message in the most final rendition he would be able to give. What, then, is the pith he now believes can convey, despite the irrelevance widely ascribed to it, the "essential relevance" of the Christian message? The existentialist protest of twentieth-century art and literature was providential in disclosing the human problem. But existentialism is definitely not the answer. At this point we lean forward suspensefully with Tillich's audience three decades ago. For who would claim this climactic question is less in need of clarifying now than it was then? On the contrary, are not multitudes of seekers and quite unsure Christians more at sea today than those who stared up, doubtfully and hopefully, at the venerable lecturer of 1963? He now has left about an hour to make his case for the Gospel.

Swiftly Tillich abbreviates Tillich in eight major chords, beginning with the Christ event's historical actuality. From his student days this had intrigued him. Jesus Christ, as really having happened, is the linchpin of Christian relevancy for every time and place, in spite of the rife ambiguities of the churches. It is noteworthy that Tillich is at pains to assert forthrightly the historicity of the Christian foundation, for it was ever and again a controverted point as his career unfolded. Even now he is accused of forfeiting the Jesus of history for a mythical Christ. The mischievous joke is still around that when told Jesus' bones were found, disproving the Resurrection, Tillich exclaimed, "Then he really lived!?" Bravo that the Earl Lectures, risen from their own grave, can debunk that parody. But there was a sticky problem that never went away for Tillich, or for modern theology. How is the Christ event that is decisive for faith related to objective study of Christian origins, with its threat of total skepticism? This problem has flared up once more under the impetus of new Jesus research. Tillich adapted a working solution from his mentor Martin Kaehler. What is indispensably real in Jesus—his unmatched saving power—is validated for faith through the biblical picture of the Christ.

The marrow of what is thus given as faith's ground and norm cannot be disproved or proved by historiography. To suppose it could be swaps *faith* for *beliefs* and forces us either to scorn fundamentalism unfaithfully or to take refuge in its preternatural enclave on the playing field of historical science. Faced in the 1990s with the evocative results of Crossan and the cohort of critics, we continue to weigh whether there is a more adequate theological solution than Tillich's. He would insist we do so. But no such solution has become apparent.

The real happening of the Christ event is the sine qua non, but the saving content of the event consists—second to nothing for Tillich—in Jesus' Cross as unreserved surrender to God. Here we encounter an aspect of this very dialectical theologian that many of his detractors, intent on sentencing him for arch-liberalism, never seemed able to handle. For Tillich the final curb against pride and greed, and the ultimate enactment of unswerving faith, is the sacrificial death of Jesus. It anchors the famous Protestant Principle—"Let God be God." It glaringly exposes sin's immeasurable cost, in God's and humanity's bearing of it. It is the singular point in history, from where the believing Christian stands, that bespeaks the relativity of everything historical. Today there arises, especially from women, serious misgiving about the whole idea of an "atoning death." In the mainline churches many seem willing, as in the "culture Christianity" of a century ago, to shrug off the Cross, widening the rift with evangelicals in

America and around the world. Further, the Jesus Seminar and recent takes on "Q" and the Gospel of Thomas, by impugning the Cross as unessential to earliest Christian tradition, bring the issue to a boil. In the ensuing crisis of Christology, these lectures will again let sound the voice of one who passionately sought relevance while also knowing firsthand the triviality of modernism without the Cross.

The Cross is thus at the heart of Tillich's Gospel, and with it there is also the "New Being in Jesus as the Christ." This is his favored way of expressing at once the Resurrection, culminating grace, and the transforming power of the Spirit. To the Protestant Principle it brings the Tillichian complement of Catholic Substance. Strictly, as *Systematic Theology II* explains, the Resurrection of Christ is the indelible fusing of saving grace in all history with Jesus and his Cross. It and the Cross together form the unsplittable nucleus of the Christ event. From the beginning, grace everywhere prepares for this event, prefiguring and facilitating. In the crucified Jesus the same redemptive aim receives its climactic insignia, and is then potentiated ("raised from the dead") in saving efficacy for the whole creation. So "theology of the Cross" and "theology of the Resurrection" imply each other. Analogies to them in other religions or nonreligions are seen as part of what they, beyond themselves, exemplify with unique luminosity.

By virtue of the New Being in and through the real life and death of Jesus, there is entrusted to the church the unconditional healing words "You are accepted!" This radical blessing is the title of Tillich's best-known sermon. He liked to join with it Luther's emphatic "in spite of!" In spite of our utter worthlessness by any other reckoning, we are accepted, whoever we are, by grace alone through faith. Here Tillich's Lutheran genes manifest themselves. The heir of the Reformation testifies powerfully—against every legalism, against self-righteousness in whatever guise, against the kind of mysticism that would cure the sinner's pain by dissolving the self in God. No, we *are*; we are *guilty*; and we are *accepted*. That is Tillichian evangelism in a nutshell.

Yet unconditional acceptance (what "justification" means today) is not the whole story. It hangs upon and releases what is indubitably both the Gospel's inmost motive and its transforming energy—agape love. This may be clearer in the Earl Lectures than in Tillich's shelf of writings as a whole. First, the unconditional acceptance of the sinner (which we all are) is an act of agape in its universality and ultimacy. To say it with 1 John 4:8, "God is love." This undergirds also, of course, the reality of Jesus' Cross and Resurrection. So it catches up in a unitive crescendo the first four chords in Tillich's resume of the Christian message. But, as we accept our acceptance, something further happens. Even the hardest-hearted are burst in upon by the love that God is. Apart from any possible self-justification, we perceive our absolute need for a Primordial Love that—because it stipulates no attainment on anyone's part—can and does reach out healingly for everyone. By the dynamism of that love, its logic and its impact, the reign of quantity and manipulation is broken. Walls of hostility—heavenward, horizontally, interiorly— begin coming down. Agape is spread abroad in our hearts and in our world as we are grasped by the God who loves and enables us to love as Jesus loved. Tillich, who plumbed psychotherapy more than most theologians did, and who carried on a ministry of informal counseling, was convinced that transformation can and must follow loving acceptance. He claimed for Christianity no monopoly on the outworking of love. Yet he could attest no standard of agape so pure as that bound up with Jesus and his Cross. At this inner nub his theology, like H. Richard Niebuhr's, is personal confession.

Well befitting modernity's splintered global village, a further chord in Christianity's relevance is its inexhaustible capacity to embrace and unite. This is not different from love, but is a distinctive application of love to the pluralism and discords of human history. Tillich was an authentic pioneer in sensing the wider ecumenical thrust of the Christian message. Heaven help us should reactionary Christianity prove him wrong! He knew the recalcitrant spirit all too painfully, but over against it he envisaged a religion of Christ free to transcend any cultural fixation. As W. E. Hocking held two generations ago, essential Christianity can undergo creative reconception, by the Holy Spirit which leads onward "into all the truth" (John

16:13). Thus Tillich sees Christianity enabled to receive into itself what he calls the vertical, the circular, and the horizontal line: which is to say, religious transcendence, classical humanism, and modern historical progressivism. Not only, then, can and must faith be affirmed as grounding science (with Michael Polanyi), but science can be affirmed as serving the vision of faith. Even technology's controlling knowledge, *pace* Heidegger, can in principle be baptized, so far as it promotes humane purposes. The untold benefits so ambiguously mingled with the rapacious downside of industrial society would thereby be harnessed to justice and love. Thus there is a utopian element in Tillich that stops short of utopianism. It balances, and is balanced by, his deep awareness of sin. By the same token Christianity can indeterminately break through the entrapment of its own historic sexism, racism, and classism. It is open to the other and the new, seeking the reunion of the separated, even while categorically respectful of the other's freedom. For Tillich this meant mutually receptive dialogue with other religions. Of course, Buddhists would hardly agree with his limited perception of their tradition(s), as he knew. But his incisive intuition that biblical faith stands in a distinctive way for the eternal significance of personal creativity has not been superseded—or for the most part appropriated—even in the current dialogues. Moreover, his courageous engagement of other commitments, both critical and accepting, still offers a worthy model for the wider ecumenical enterprise.

In the Earl Lectures, among numerous other

motifs pulled in as needed from the encyclopedic sweep of Tillich's thought, a further main chord that merits special attention is universal salvation. Unquestionably this greatly bolsters in our time a religion's relevance. In church history Origen is remembered for espousing the *apokatastasis panton*—the eternal "restoration of all things" in God; for more than a millennium it was cited against him as heterodox. But in modern theology a suasive call has been arising to believe in "good hope for all" (Schleiermacher). As Karl Rahner stresses, the Christian God "desires everyone to be saved" (1 Tim. 4:2), and the seeming reluctance of orthodox churches to agree has prompted abhorrence among humanists of all stripes. In *Systematic Theology III* Tillich saliently affirmed the nonextinction beyond death of the individual in community and repudiated as demonic the splitting of eternal destinies between heaven and hell. This surprised some who doubted he held a view of everlasting life. These skeptics had overlooked how elemental for Tillich is the goodness of creation. All finite potentials root in God, fall from God in the tragic outworking of temporal freedom, and return again to God eschatologically with the fruit of their freedom. If anything, the lectures before us are more universal than the published system, for they unabashedly affirm the divine source and end of even the most negative creativity of history (symbolized for Origen in the redemption of Satan). This may show the increasing impact of Buddhism, with its unmitigated—though impersonal—universalism. However, in Barth's theology too there was occurring an unlimited "triumph of grace." It is a theme that seems peculiarly appointed to rectify, on the most ultimate tableau, the dehumanizing and desacralizing that cause, if Tillich is right, the felt irrelevance of Christian preaching.

Beyond these seven relevance-begetting leitmotifs—historicity, Cross, New Being, acceptance, agape love, unifying openness, and eternal fruition for all—is a further chord in the Earl Lectures that undergirds and conjoins the others. This is God godself, our ultimate concern, the axis of meaning and the primordial mystery. It was H. Richard Niebuhr who said, in reviewing *Systematic Theology I*, that Tillich's theology was great theology because the sense of God in it was great. That sense or consciousness of God pervades this little, long-delayed book with undiminished vitality, but there are also some surprising twists. Tillich's distinct kind of God-talk was famous and also infamous for making so much of the "Ground of Being," his metaphor for Being-itself. It would have amazed him that the metaphor eventually found its way into some Christian hymns; he had advised not using it devotionally. Meanwhile "Being-itself," while helpful to many, was under furious assault from both process theology, for freezing God into changeless substance, and analytic philosophy, for reifying a mere participle into Something real. Those bombarding Tillich paid scant heed to the rethinking he steadily did as he carefully listened, or to the full orchestration of his God-concept as it unfolded in the third systematics volume. Hardly any notice was taken of his demotion of "Being" from the one literal to a symbolic expression of the Divine, nor did his seminal exposition of the Trinity make a large splash. The fact is, however, that Being as a formal concept plays a quite reduced role in the culminating phase of Tillich's reflections. He learned from process and analytic thinkers, whether or not they learned from him, and it is not a superficial garnish when he winds up Volume III by naming his standpoint "eschatological panentheism." In that volume the paramount image is the eternal and temporal Spiritual Presence who mediates and consummates the work of the Creative Ground and the Reconciling Christ. Strands of all this interlace the Earl Lectures, with notable accent on the nonobjectifiability of the biblical God, omniactive and always sovereignly free. We may surmise the *term* "Spirit" is not used in the lectures because it would have added semantic complexity untenable within the all too limited frame. But the twofold *meaning* of Spirit is palpably here in the transformative open-endedness of the New Being and the integrating fulfillment of all things in God.

IV

These lectures do not by a long shot refer to everything in Tillich, but they are a rich and fascinating résumé. They can be a lively tonic for any who may have sealed the celebrated and controversial giant into stereotypes of earlier moments of his thought. They should also prompt many first visits to the unexhausted lodes of his writing. The ore there will surely be mined for a long time to come, since in some ways—like the wider ecumenism—the world is just beginning to catch up with Tillich, and there are no obvious ways it has left him behind. The tensions in his thought, like that between history and historiography, or between prophetic judgment and universal redemption, or between technology as controlling tyrant and as humane servant, will be helpfully stoked up. For the internal problems of Tillich have yet to be parsed empathetically and adequately. To explore these problems will never be dull, or at all irrelevant to existing on the boundaries of church and world. For the fault lines in Tillich, as well as the aquifers of his inspiration, coincide with those that endure and emerge in the Christian adventure overall. This must be why this happily salvaged manifesto can incite the feeling that the churches of Christ, with all that is awesome and appalling in their history, are just now facing some of their most spine-tingling challenges as the third millennium dawns.

Durwood Foster
Berkeley, California

The Irrelevance
and Relevance of the
Christian Message for
Humanity Today

PAUL
TILLICH

I T WAS A GREAT HONOR to be chosen as Earl Lecturer at the Pacific School of Religion, where twice previously I had the pleasure to teach in the summer school. Moreover, the annual pastoral conference is a particularly significant setting for this series of lectures. When asked by the Earl Committee to give them a subject, and I thought about all the possible subjects on which I have spoken or written, suddenly it came to me like a voice of conscience: "You must speak in this situation, not what you already know, or believe you know—of course, you know nothing—but what is nearest your heart, what lies on your conscience." Then, when I thought about it, I decided that what worries me most deeply in these last years is the question: "Is the Christian message (especially the Christian preaching) still relevant to the people of our time? And if not, what is the cause of this? And does that reflect on the message of Christianity itself?" Out of these questions my subject matter arose. Therefore do not take what follows here so much as a new intellectual discovery, but rather as a personal confession of a deep worry concerning our churches, our theology, and my own work.

1

The Avowed Irrelevance of Christian Preaching to the Contemporary World

Almost day and night there comes to my ears violent complaint about the irrelevance of Christian preaching. Of course, this is not a completely new thing. Something like it has affected the theological endeavors of two millennia. These endeavors, back to the period of the Apologists, are interesting not only for the historian of theology. And they have not only the function (which Luther recognized) of protecting the Christian church against alien intrusions. Let me try to put them in an additional light, namely that of the question: "How can the message of Christianity be communicated?" If we do this we might discover it brings new insight into the work of Christian thinkers over two thousand years. This work has already clearly started with the Fourth Gospel, where we have, not a history of the life of Jesus, but an interpretation of this life making it relevant to the Hellenistic setting of the Christian communities. Or think of the theologians who were called the Apologists because they answered the questions of the pagan world. They wanted to make Christianity relevant to the educated of that world. Or take a great mind like Origen, who in his theology tried to make the Gospel relevant for the Eastern church. Or Augustine, who on different presuppositions in a quite different situation, made it immensely relevant for the Western church. Again, take the greatest constructive theologian of the Middle Ages, Thomas Aquinas, who had to speak to a period in which the feudalism of princes and city aristocracy was at its height. Or think of Ockham, who had to express the Christian message again in a quite new way to the dawning awareness of the modern individual as individual. Or think of another line of development: the so-called German Mystics, and before them the Franciscan Order. Consider Francis himself, who tried in a new way to make the church relevant to the masses of the poor.

Then there was the Reformation, which tried to make the Gospel speak to the princes of the empire and to the increasingly personalized people of the city and its special social groups. Then let us jump to the Enlightenment's radical attempt in the eighteenth century to adapt Christianity to the newly recovered power of reason—reason in the sense of the fundamental principles of knowledge, of ethics, aesthetics, of politics, and of all realms of humanity's spiritual functions. Then—perhaps a little provincially—let me point to what I like to call the "great synthesis," the bringing together of all elements of culture in two men: from the philosophical side in Hegel and German classical philosophy, and in Schleiermacher, the father of modern Protestant theology. The very title of Schleiermacher's famous "Speeches to the Despisers of Christianity"[1] shows that he wanted to address the problem of these lectures, namely to make Christianity relevant again to the educated classes of his period. Now when the great synthesis did not succeed—it was a superhuman attempt which broke down—there came the self-restriction of the Kantian philosophy, in correlation with the victorious European bourgeoisie of the middle and later nineteenth century. And towards the end of the century there was the attempt of the religious socialists and the Social Gospel theologians in America to answer in the name of Christianity to the social problems of the masses.

These thinkers and movements have become chapters in the history of Christian thought. In terms of my theme, I propose looking at them as bearers of the history of trying to make the Christian message relevant to the always changing human situation. But there is another line of thought that is uncharacteristic of most of the theologians I have named. This different line says: in order to make the Christian message relevant, one must emphasize its wholly otherness. The phrase "wholly other" (*ganz anders* in German) was used by the renowned theologian—my colleague when I taught at Marburg—Rudolf Otto. His book *The Idea of the Holy* describes with a vast amount of material the radical otherness of the holy. Similarly, the opposing line of thought, which contrasts with most of the theologians cited earlier, holds that we must show the otherness of the Christian message, whatever the situation may be. Those taking this position are the "theologians of offense," to use a Kierkegaardian term. They contrast with those I would call the "theologians of mediation." These latter mediate between the Christian message and every particular cultural situation, while the theologians of offense sharpen the opposition of the message to every situation.

The theology of offense goes back to Tertullian's "I believe because it is absurd" (*credo quia absurdum est*). He never said this, but some of his ideas could be joined into such a phrase. Another theologian of offense was the great Athanasius, who was victorious over Greek methods of thinking. Similarly the mystic Bernard of Clairvaux fought against the dialectical "Yes and No" of Abelard. Although better known to many because of his relationship with Heloise, Abelard was a towering representative of theological mediation. Bernard won at the time, but Abelard has had a larger influence through the centuries. The theology of offense becomes manifest again in Luther's battle with Erasmus, and we can see it today in irrational sectarian movements. It shows up in theological fundamentalism and in primitive aggressive biblicism. But Kierkegaard, from whom I take the word "offense," is the most characteristic example up till today. Karl Barth, with his famous "No!" against any mediation, is one point in the line.

It is interesting that offending and mediating were always used together, and sometimes by the same theologian. Tertullian, who provided key slogans for the theology of offense, was at the same time the first to translate the Greek philosophical terms of Christian dogma into Latin, and to fight for this. Or consider Augustine, who combines neoplatonic philosophy and the Christian offense. Calvin, again, was a most radical theologian of offense, and, on the other hand, much more rational in his way of thinking than Luther was.

It seems to me that both ways of thinking are needed by the Christian church in this world, but both have their dangers of making Christianity irrelevant. The theology of mediation runs the risk of complete estrangement from the original message. On the other hand, the theology of offense may deny any relationship. The first becomes irrelevant by adaptation, the second by opposition. Both are equally dangerous if they remain alone. In talking with people about the felt irrelevance of the Christian message, I found many who said the reason is that it has no relationship to our situation. But, surprisingly, I also found many who said it does not communicate because it does not have the power of offense, which belongs to everything divine. Thus mediation and offense must *both* be kept alive in Christian preaching and teaching.

Although America is the "country of new beginnings," and usually does not care much about past history, I always try to sketch the antecedents of the present situation. For it is necessary to realize that not everything confronting us is really a new beginning. It may well have a long and powerful tradition from which much can be learned. In the ancient church the theological efforts we have considered were first of all missionary. One wanted to win over the Greeks, or more exactly members of the Hellenistic culture which embraced the whole Mediterranean and far beyond it. In the Middle Ages the interest in making the message relevant was to grasp and integrate social classes that previously were not participant subjects in the faith of the larger society. In the Enlightenment one wanted to come to terms with reason, whatever this word meant; and in classical German philosophy one wanted to combine all elements of modern times.

Today, however, something new has happened. The contemporary question is whether we are entering—or have already entered—a post-Christian period. This question has been raised surprisingly often, for many people think Christianity cannot adapt itself to the radically new world. If instead of adaptation the method of offense is used, then we may have—as the evangelicals do—a transitory psychological effect, but not a fundamental transformation.

This situation is responsible for the seriousness with which the problem is being taken inside and outside the churches. It is widely recognized by the churchly institutions, but even more sharply by three types of individuals who have different relations to the churches. The first are active members of the church, including many ministers, who ask hiddenly of themselves, sometimes to friends and colleagues, very rarely to the congregations, the question of a post-Christian era. The second type I have found worried in this way are people at the edge of the church. They are still concerned but not centrally active in the church because they feel their religious life is not satisfied by its irrelevant activities. Then there are people outside the church whom one could call (and I say this out of much experience) disappointed lovers of Christianity. The latter two types are very vocal, and not out of aggressiveness but out of distress. I believe their criticism is more important than that from persons who are completely estranged, from enemies or cynics. Of course, often those who are entirely outside do see the situation more clearly than those who still have ties with Christianity. But more often they lack any real understanding of what is going on in the religious realm. Nevertheless, they too must be heard by those who try to make Christianity relevant for those inside and outside the churches. Thus I made it a principle of my whole vocational life to listen to them eagerly—to find out why they not only deem Christianity irrelevant but totally deny it.[2] In any case, it is encouraging that the churches have become officially and earnestly concerned about the possibility of a post-Christian period.

The Roman church, especially the present pope, are examples of this.[3] The uneasiness about the dogma of papal infallibility cannot be concealed. Rome's main concern, however, is with the increasingly felt irrelevance of the liturgical and ethical practice which is at the heart of its institutional life.

In Protestantism the main concern is the irrelevance of preaching. There is a widespread feeling that the typical preaching does not reach large groups of people, even among those who regularly attend church. This appears to be the case in spite of a considerable number of good—even brilliant—preachers, and in spite of increased membership and attendance, and in general the apparent resurgence of religion since World War II. Protestantism, of course, has no central leadership like the papacy. But there is shared concern among many Protestants about the phenomenon my colleague in Chicago, Gibson Winter, has called the "suburban captivity of the churches."[4] This is certainly one of the factors contributing to the church's irrelevancy. It is recognized that the relevance of the preaching is not proved by habitual attendance, since that has largely sociological reasons—of status, desire to belong, or ingrained feelings of religious duty. Such factors do not mean the message of the church is relevant for the people. Often they simply need to participate in a socially significant act. These are a few of the insights church leaders have been gaining into the problem of relevancy. I am extremely grateful for every salient voice that promotes a consciousness of these matters.

Now let me consider more concretely the manifestations of the irrelevance of the Christian message today. It is not the task of this first chapter to address the causes. They will be explored in the following chapter. But after having lifted up the awareness, I next turn to the manifestations. This may have the disadvantage, as I go from point to point, of conveying a very negative attitude toward the church or toward Christianity. I do not shy away from giving this impression, because I believe, if we do not take up the heavy burden these manifestations of irrelevancy put upon us, we cannot joyfully say yes to the church with honesty. Therefore I ask you to follow me in a painful but necessary task.

But what is relevance? Everyone knows such a word in its usual sense, but we must ask more exactly for its meaning in the context of our problem. In that context "relevant" means that the Christian message answers the existential questions of the humanity of today. "Irrelevant" means it does not answer those questions. By "existential" questions I refer to those which concern the *whole* of human existence: not only knowing, but also feeling and willing—all sides of our being as they come together in the center of the personality. Some examples of these questions are: What is the meaning of my being, and of all being of which I am a part? What does it mean to be a human being in a world full of evil in body and mind, in individual and society? Where do I get the courage to live? How can I save my personal being amid the mechanized ways of life? How can I have hope? And for what? How can I overcome the conflicts that torture me inwardly? Where can I find an ultimate concern that overcomes my emptiness and has the power to transform? These are existential questions. They could also be called passionate quests for a meaningful life. Is Christian preaching, as it is done today, able to answer these questions and longings for a healing message?

Let us also be clear what is meant by the "humanity of today." By this phrase we refer to those human beings who exist fully in the structures of the life of our time and have the kind of questions just considered—often consciously, perhaps more often unconsciously. This does not include, of course, all people who are presently alive. Many are not yet fully under the power of the structures of modern existence. But those who are in the grip of these powers and who have what I have called existential questions, *they* are the ones who characterize and shape our period. If the Christian message cannot be relevant any longer for them, the post-Christian era has started. For these—rather than the pre-moderns or the satisfied who think they need no healing—are those whom the Sermon on the Mount calls the "poor in spirit."[5]

It is with a certain fear and trembling that I propose the following symptoms of the irrelevance today of the Christian message. For my impressions may be only partial, and important data may have been overlooked. Please consider what is given here as examples, to be corrected by your own better information and larger experience. I will accept your judgment.

The first of my six examples is the irrelevance of the Christian language. Regarding the existential questions raised above, one can immediately see that the repetition of biblical, creedal, or liturgical language has no significance for those who ask them. The original power of the great Christian symbols is lost. Originally they answered questions. Now they are stumbling blocks to be believed by tradition and authority. Compounding the problem is the confusion between faith and belief. Faith is the state of being grasped by something that has ultimate meaning, and acting and thinking on the basis of this as a centered person. Beliefs are opinions held to be true, which may or may not really be true. We need beliefs in practical affairs all the time. But they are never a matter of life and death. One of the worst things making the Christian message irrelevant is the identification of faith with belief in doctrines. Especially bad is the demand to believe what is unbelievable. It would greatly help to use in all our preaching the gift of the English language—not available, for example, in German or French—of the *two* words "faith" and "belief." We need to say clearly that faith is being grasped by a power that concerns us ultimately, and belief is being not certain, but accepting something preliminary.[6]

The modern person's impossibility to understand the language of the tradition is true of almost all Christian symbols. They have lost the power to pierce the soul: to make restless, anxious, desperate, joyful, ecstatic, accepting of meaning. A salient illustration is the soft-spoken, emaciated, sentimentalized Jesus whose picture hangs in Sunday schools and side rooms of churches. This sentimental Jesus has nothing to say to the strong in our period. But beyond this, the word "Jesus" does not communicate in depth anymore. And the word "Christ," which originally meant the anointed one sent by God to bring the new aeon, has become unununderstandable. It is used as a proper name, instead of the paradox of a climactic function given to a human being. The same kind of thing is true of the language of the sacraments. They were always secondary in Protestantism anyway, and could become effective again only if we should once more live in a period where the whole world is perceived sacramentally: as an expression of the creative divine ground, the divine presence in everything. For someone like Bonaventura, the great thirteenth-century Franciscan, everything in the world was a symbol, and thus sacramental understanding was possible. It could be today, in spite of all mechanization, if the sense for the symbolic were recovered. But in the half-dead liturgies of the Protestant churches what can the sacraments really mean for the members, except perhaps community action and what is preached along with them?

The second example of the irrelevance today of Christian preaching is its content. Typically, for Protestantism at least, it is the Law that is predominant. The teachings of Jesus are offered as centering in and confirming his moral commandments. These are supposed to be more elevated than the Mosaic commandments. But they have lost the character of breaking through all Law. They have lost the essence of what gospel originally meant—

16

the "good news" that a new reality is present, which gives before it demands, which accepts before it transforms. This loss has caused the replacement of pastoral care by psychotherapeutic counseling—though I am glad to note that nowadays many ministers already as students learn from psychotherapy that you cannot use the Law to transform anyone. You first must accept and then you can transform. More generally, the lack of distinctive religious content in today's preaching tends to make what the New Testament calls the "assembly of God" (*ecclesia*) into a club for social activities. Some of these are worthwhile, some utterly superfluous. In any case the minister, as director of these activities, has little time for study and the preparation of the sermon—or for counseling with the innumerable individuals in our time who are in trouble.[7] These go to the secular analysts or to nobody. Occasionally the question of relevancy comes up, and one asks whether the club activities could not be sponsored by any ethical group. Why have the church, if that is all it does?

The third example of irrelevance is especially important. It is the traditionalist attitude towards the Christian tradition held widely among laity and ministers. Tradition is good. Traditionalism is bad. The traditionalist attitude toward the tradition stops one from asking for the living meaning of its elements. They are taken for granted and not questioned any longer. But only if the tradition is being transformed again and again can it be saved as a living reality. A deadly consequence of tradi-

17

tionalism is the avoiding of serious issues. It seems that ministerial conferences tend to avoid basic theological problems. In a time in which all fundamentals of Christianity are under attack, such avoidance sharply increases the irrelevance. Ministers who freely discuss basic problems of faith in preaching, teaching, and counseling, are often threatened with loss of their jobs. Moreover, it is especially distressing when Sunday school teachers who are interesting (which sometimes happens!)—because they address questions which are in the minds of the children—face accusations by parents, or even dismissal, while those are safe who counter such questions with "You must believe!" Few things have contributed as much to the irrelevance of Christianity as has the Sunday school. Something which aids and abets traditionalism is the expectation by many lay persons that the churches should be a mainstay of conformism and conservatism in general. They forget that, once upon a time, there existed the prophets of Israel, and that in the whole history of Christianity—not to mention Jesus and the Apostles—revolutionary reformers again and again took the pivotal steps in developing the churches. To many, controversy about fundamentals seems to weaken the foundation on which one stands. This is so not only in the churches. Overall now the word "controversial" has become a negative one. But it should be a most positive word. For in controversies, in "yes and no," the truth can be known, and in no other way. If controversial statements are excluded—be it from the church, be it from society—then this church and this society are condemned to slow decay.

A fourth example of irrelevance concerns the personalities of ministers and typical church-goers. What the church needs in any period (and got through much of its history) is leadership by the strongest, most dynamic, and most daring kinds of people—those in whom there is high vitality balanced with profound spirituality. That is the ideal leader in the church, lay or clergy. Today such leadership is rare, since the strongest go into the creative functions of culture where they see the greatest opportunities. Of course, there is a "sacred weakness," of which Paul says: "Where I am weak, I am strong."[8] But this weakness, as Paul himself shows in every word and in every moment of his life, has nothing to do with weakness in vitality and lack of creative strength. If one says asceticism is necessary in the church, and perhaps sacrifice of vitality, I answer: "Asceticism is valuable only if it is not the result of a natural or induced inability to affirm life—only if it is the sacrifice of something really strong which is there."

Vitality does not mean athletic vitality. A fragile body can have the highest world-changing vitality, as we see in Paul or in a person like Pascal. Pushing religion into the emotional realm either to save it, by those who wish it well, or to get rid of it, as outsiders may desire, is a sure road to irrelevance. In the German churches it was the lack of males and young people which showed the irrelevancy of the Christian message.[9] Only those emotionally receptive to revivalism and evangelism were listening. But emotion does not last. If Christianity is not relevant any longer to the strong "male mind"—to use a phrase nowadays unfitting—then there is not much hope it can regain its relevancy. If religion is pushed into an emotional corner where it has no impact on thinking and action, it will disappear.

As the fifth example, there is the vast irrelevance of the Christian message for various social classes. Perhaps most removed from Christianity are the radical labor movement and the intelligentsia, or so it was in Germany. It is somewhat different in the United States and Great Britain. Least removed are the lower middle classes, the farmers, some elements of the upper classes, and numbers of the disinherited classes or races. Most problematic in this sociological survey are the organizational middle classes: the "organization man," the executives and officials. The irrelevance of Christianity for industrial labor, more in Europe than America, is based primarily on the fact that labor was the first victim in the process of "humans becoming mere things," to be discussed in the next chapter. As for the intelligentsia, in it all the causal factors we shall be considering are elevated into consciousness. For the tradition-bound lower middle class and the farmers, religion tends to remain an established custom, and often is a deeper way of living. The upper classes too—for instance, the European aristocracy—are customarily religious.

In part there is internal acceptance, and in part they are interested economically and politically to keep religion alive in the masses, as a barrier to change. In the disinherited classes and races, Christianity is relevant, but in an irrational and often primitive superstitious form. Finally, in the organizational middle classes, religious habits are often carried over from lower middle class roots. Partly they become a matter of proper status or, worse, of polite indifference.

The sixth and last example of Christianity's irrelevance has to do with interest and passion. It was Hegel who said that without these nothing great occurs in history. I have in mind the small amount of interest and passion our society invests in Christianity, as compared with what goes into the creative activities of other realms of culture. The comparison is very distressing. There is tremendous passion and interest in science, in the techniques of space exploration, in the political question of East and West, and in survival. One may mention also the struggle of ideologies, the problem of overpopulation, victory over major diseases, the competition of psychoanalytic schools, the development of secular universities, the theatre, the novel, all of the arts, even philosophy, if it deals with relevant issues. All eyes look at these things. Very few look at the churches—except when they have tragic and ridiculous heresy trials, or express an awareness of their irrelevance, as at the Second Vatican Council.

Now in spite of all the manifestations of its irrelevance, there are individuals for whom the Christian message remains infinitely significant. It is the reward of ministry and of theological work to serve these people, whether in theological thinking or in person-to-person priesthood. This continues in a large way. But is that enough? In most periods of the church, more was intended and was attained. The universal relevance of the Christian message was grounded in the human situation. Can that be reestablished for our present world? If the answer, often given with great hesitation, is yes, then the question is how? And here again arises the issue I posed. Which is most important, the way of offense, or the way of mediation? But to answer, we must know the *causes* of the irrelevance we have described. If the cause is the desire, as many preachers say, to escape God—to avoid God's presence, in dread of God's judgment and grace— then only the answer of offense is needed. But if the cause results from our providential situation in history, then the mediating answer is required. Now rather than decide for the one or the other, we might find a way to unite them, and I believe we must. What is crucial, however, even if many readers have more concrete information and would give examples different from mine, is that we must take the problem of irrelevance in its full weight upon our minds and hearts.

2

The Nature of Present-Day Thought: Its Strangeness to Traditional Christianity

At the end of the first chapter I put before you a problem: What are the *causes* of the irrelevance of the Christian message for people today? The question of causes largely determines the answer to my other questions: What does this irrelevance mean for the future of Christianity, and what can Christianity do about it? Should the response to the irrelevance be what I called "mediation," or should it be what I called "giving offense"? I will leave it to each of you to decide this for your situation, but my own answer will be that the basic issue in the present situation is that of mediation. Nevertheless, the mediation must have within it elements one could call offense or attack or controversy.

What are the principles determining the modern mind? Much has been written about it, and many of you are acquainted with the factors I want to mention. But I will place them now in the context of our present subject: the irrelevance and the relevance of the Christian message. As an initial example I propose the symbol of space exploration. It seems to me not only the most current but also the most characteristic of the traits of the modern mind. It is not the beginning of something, but rather the extreme instance of a long development. In extreme cases one often sees better what the general tendency is than one does in more ambiguous cases. So let us take space exploration as something symbolizing the modern mind generally. It contains four elements. I will first sketch them briefly and then go more fully into their emergence.

The first is the emphasis on the horizontal dimension of life: on the dimension of going ahead in time and space endlessly; going ahead in the world which is determined by time and space, causality and substance (and other categories); and going ahead in this world indefinitely, without any termination. This is the first point to keep in mind in trying to understand the present situation.

The second is the intention to control nature. Space exploration has been rightly considered a technical miracle—"miracle" taken in a more metaphoric than exact sense of the word. The fact that it has achieved one thing never dreamt of in former centuries, breaking through the bondage of the earth's gravity, is something which indeed approaches the imagination of possible miracles in former periods. But if one asks, "Control nature for what?" then it is hard to find an answer, especially among those who do the controlling. They accomplish something which was an end for their work, such as shooting substances of the earth into space to learn about it. But the learning becomes the means for another end, to go ahead again. And if this is reached, it again becomes a means for some further end. This is the second characteristic of the modern mind.

The third is something intrinsic to science: making everything into calculable objects which can be described in terms of numbers. Things describable in terms of numbers can be managed, divided, and put together again. They have lost their meaning for themselves. They have become nothing but tools to be handled by a human subject. This is especially clearly expressed in space exploration. The earth itself has become an object at which the astronaut looks down. More than ever, it has lost what it formerly meant for humanity: the quality of being the nourishing mother, nourishing and swallowing back what she has produced (as with the mother goddesses, and in the feeling towards earth still existing in pre-modern humankind). But for modernity this has disappeared. Human being is now above even the gravitation field of the earth and looks back at it. This is the arch symbol of controlling what originally was mother. So it is with all things between heaven and earth. It is everywhere the same. The connecting love, the *eros,* as Plato calls it, or the *philia,* the friendship to things, has been translated into calculating subjection of all the realities of the world. This is the third characteristic of the modern mind symbolized in space exploration.

Finally, there is the reduced concept of reason one could call "calculating reason." Reason was not always the tool simply of the business man, the technician, or of scientific analysis. It was formerly the

25

power of knowing the ultimate principles of the good, the true, and the beautiful. This traditional concept of reason has been lost since the middle of the nineteenth century. It has been replaced by something which in former centuries was only secondary: humanity's rational power for control. This is the fourth characteristic expressed in space exploration as symbolizing the modern mind.

But now a warning is in order, especially for American audiences. Do not believe what space exploration symbolizes is completely new. It has a long development behind it and a great development. To understand ourselves it is always necessary to go back. I know that America is a country of the "new beginning." This is in the blood and nerves of every born American. But what is supposed to be a new beginning is often only a last step of a very old development. This is certainly the case with the four points mentioned in space exploration as symbolizing the modern mind. The present situation is the result of many steps made by Western humanity since the Renaissance of the fifteenth and sixteenth centuries. A kind of scholarly conscience obliges me to go back a few centuries before returning to our present moment of triumphant space exploration.

The Renaissance is not what it is often called—rebirth of the ancient traditions. It means rather, in the religious sense of "born again," the rebirth of Western society in all respects: religious, cultural, and political. Of course, it is a rebirth with the help of the ancient sources of Mediterranean civilization, the classical Greek and Latin writers and the biblical literature. In this process the ancient traditions were transformed in many respects, due to the Christian background of the Renaissance. However pagan it tried to behave, it was largely without success. And whoever since then tried to behave pagan in the Western world did so without success. They were always dependent on the fundamental Christian substance of Western culture. But one of the most important transformations that did take place in the Renaissance was the turn from the Greek contemplative and the medieval transcendent ideals of life to a third possible ideal: that of actively controlling and shaping the world. This implied a high valuation of technical sciences and the beginning of that fertile interaction between pure and applied sciences that contributes immensely to the ongoing development of both. This interaction of science and technology did not exist in Greece, or in late antiquity or the Middle Ages. It was something new which appeared in the Renaissance.

There are three archetypal symbols which can be useful for our overview of the fundamental attitudes of Western civilization: the circle, the vertical line, and the horizontal line. For the world of classical antiquity the magical symbol is the circle: the fulfillment of life *within* the cosmos, within the structure of the universe as philosophers and scientists tried to describe it, the fulfillment of everything potential in humanity and nature within this realm. Even time has the character of a circle, returning to itself. This is the one root symbol. We find it confirmed in every expression of the Greek mind, including the sculpture and the architecture.

Then, in the late ancient world—Hellenistic in contrast to Greek—something quite new appears. There is a breaking through of the circle of the cosmos. Instead of remaining within the circle there is a driving vertically upward, trying to transcend the cosmos, to reach the ultimate itself in meaning and being. This becomes determinative for the whole of late antiquity and the middle ages. It is the vertical line, which aspires to rise beyond the universe to the divine, the sublime and supreme.

Then there is the third archetypyal symbol: the horizontal line. This is the trend ahead, toward controlling and transforming the given world: either in the service of God, as in the Calvinist Reformation, or in the service of humanity, as in the Enlightenment. I hold that this emergence of the horizontal line in the Renaissance and Reformation is the first step of a development of which space exploration is the provisional last step. A new feeling for reality arises in modern Western humanity. Reality is not that which is to be understood and contemplated. Nor is it that which is left below when we elevate toward the ultimate, the union with God. Reality is rather that which, on the basis of knowledge, is to be controlled. In this horizontal line we have to go ahead and ahead.

These things were supported by the astronomy of the Renaissance. It raised the earth from the place of darkness and heaviness to the dignity of a star. And this was supported by Renaissance literature with its ideals of utopian social justice and nature controlled to fulfill human desire. The heavenly utopia as traditionally imagined was transformed into an earthly one. "Utopia" means something hoped for which so far has no place in reality. The hope now became, not fulfillment above, but in time and space. This lifted the importance of technology, compared with pure science, far above what was possible in classical Greece and the intervening periods. A symbol for this is Leonardo, who combined the Renaissance ideal of human fulfillment with studies of empirical phenomena—with an endless curiosity for everything happening in nature. With this he further joined technical experimentation, especially with a military focus—just as today weapons research plays so large a role in developing technology.

Now we ask: Under the control of the horizontal line, so typical for modernity, what becomes of the vertical line—the line towards what transcends the cosmos? There is a man, Pascal, who contributed (as one of the greatest mathematicians) much to the situation I described, but who also realized what was lost—the vertical line. He tried to regain this line towards the divine and ultimate. In an ecstatic way, in mystical experience, Pascal rejected the god of those philosophers who identified the cosmos with atoms in motion. He affirmed instead the God of Abraham, Isaac, and Jacob. And this very touching thing is a counter-symbol to the exploration of space today. The same man who helped to make this exploration possible saw already in the seventeenth century what was lost and tried to find it again. But the development followed the horizontal line. In the eighteenth century the belief in progress, and in the nineteenth belief in universal evolution, supported the industrial, social, and political revolutions which shaped the modern world. Of course, there were always attempts to recover the vertical line. Romantics, mystics, classicists wanted to return to an earlier world, and there are those who want this even today. When I was professor at Frankfurt in the early '30s there was a group there who earnestly believed that both the modern horizontal line and the medieval vertical line have to be overcome by the circle of classical Greece. But history proved stronger than their longing to look again at the eternal essences rather than anticipate a humanly created future. The latter prevailed, and prevails till today.

In the new way of thinking one of the primary religious shocks was the removal of humanity and the earth from the cosmic center. In the biblical literature, and through 1500 years of church history up to the Renaissance, the earth was at the center of the universe. Human history was the ultimate aim of the earth's creation, and the Christ was the center of human history. Therefore, in religious people, the Renaissance raised the urgent question: What about the position of humanity in the providential acting of God? What about the cosmic significance of Christ so often emphasized in the Bible? Does not removing the earth from the center undercut the significance of humanity and the Christ? Is not the whole drama of salvation reduced to a series of happenings on a small planet at a particular time without universal meaning? All this questioning long preceded the start of space exploration. It pervades our present situation and is the fundamental cause for the irrelevance of Christian preaching today.

But there is one point which has fully appeared only in the last decade. This is the management—the control—not only of the earth in its subhuman elements, but of humanity itself by human beings. Humans are made into objects, and nothing other than objects, in a medical, psychological, and sociological sense. Not only are the moods, vitality, and emotions of a person transformed by drugs, but to a large extent the person as well. And to transform a personality by chemical means is the complete objectification—the making into a calculable object—of the one who is the subject of all calculation. At Harvard there is what we call "Skinnerism"—Professor Skinner's psychological attempt to force humanity into an ideal utopia.[1] The Renaissance envisaged such a utopia, without the thought of force. But now humanity is to be forced to its happiness. Christian theology was wiser than this. It always held that even God cannot force humans to eternal happiness. The human always can resist. Skinner does not think so. He believes it is possible to bring humanity into a state of happiness where even the desire to reject God or fellow humans or happiness is extinguished. But that would produce, not a happy human being, but a blessed animal. Such is exactly the aim of Skinnerism. However, in a less radical way, we have the same intention in the mass management of humans symbolized in the corporations. We have it in the psychologically subtle management of people through advertising. In all such cases we have the attempt to transform persons into controllable objects. The same persons may have some red Indian reservations[2] in their souls where they hear music or poetry. But these reservations have as little influence on the reality of life as those of the red Indians on the political life of this country. Thus has the human being now become an object.

If this is the kind of world in which we are presently living, how shall we react? Here I must first give a caution. Modern humanity is not simply non-Christian and even less anti-Christian. The greatest anti-Christians in recent history, like Nietzsche and Marx, show their Christian roots with every word they say. Ours is not a new world far away from Christianity. I would call it one of Christian humanism. It is humanism, but not that of Greece or India or China. It is Christian humanism. The ethical principles remain in substance Christian. Our joking talk about ourselves being "pagan," when we love nature, for example, is not absolutely serious. The famous pagan Nietzsche, or even Goethe, who has been called the great pagan, were Christian humanists. The most candid of them, Nietzsche, acknowledged this when he said he had the blood of his greatest enemies—the priests—within himself. This is the paradox of Christian humanism, of anti-Christian attitudes within the Western world, the substance of which is Christian.

What is the attitude towards life in those who can be called typically Christian humanists? They affirm life, but they do it in the Stoic and Epicurean ways, transformed into modern activism. Even the materialists follow the neo-Stoic attitudes toward life—resignation towards fate, inner superiority to vicissitudes, accepting whatever happens. This is a faith. It can also be called, in many cases, naturalistic. But it is a faith, and often a heroic faith. It heroically accepts without hope the destiny that comes upon one. And it is an attitude in which the problem and the anxiety of guilt play no role. Therefore one of the fundamental elements of Christianity is repressed, at least intentionally. I say intentionally, because I know from psychoanalyst friends that many of the most humanistic and naturalistic persons who come to them, when the analysis reaches a certain point, reveal to the analyst a profound feeling of guilt. It is repressed, but is still there and breaks out in the moment they freely express themselves. Here we have another example of what I call the Christian substance of even anti-Christian humanism. It is often an heroic acceptance of finitude, but usually connected with something the Stoics did not have: belief in the possibility to progress in actualizing human potentialities. <u>Although they have no hope in the Christian sense, they do have a hope</u>. It is based either on identifying themselves with a future realm of peace and justice—a last generation for which all hopes are fulfilled. Or it is based on identification with a group—a collective, as in communism—for whom they believe fulfillment will come, or has already partly come. Communism, seen from the viewpoint of the individual, is identification with a group which is the bearer of meaning, though the individual participates in the meaning only remotely, in self-surrender without individual hope. There is in it the spirit of heroic Stoicism. But unlike Stoicism it is not static, unhistorical, purely individualistic heroism, since it is identification with a group.

On this basis the idea of salvation, which is definitive for Christianity (making it the religion, or the irreligion,[3] of salvation) is largely equated with technical control. We should not underestimate this, because healing power belongs to salvation. <u>"Saved"</u> means literally <u>"healed."</u> Technical control, in healing, and in overcoming limits of finitude which are burdensome (like mechanical work, or like barriers of space and time) shows its saving power. This is an element in the attitude of modern humanity to the horizontal line of technical control by which it relates to its world.

What then are the points of contrast between the modern and the Christian self-interpretation of humanity? These are the direct causes for the irrelevance of the Christian message.

First of all, in Christianity, the vertical line is the basically important line. In Christian symbolism the Kingdom of God comes from above and leads above. Now it is very difficult for typical modern people to understand any longer this vertical line. The symbols expressing it, like Kingdom of God or eternal life, are ununderstandable for them. This is not only because they believe Christians must take these symbols literally and therefore absurdly, and rightly reject them for this reason. Even if they know (as I have often experienced) that theology is not as stupid as that and should not be identified with primitivism, they still feel the Christian symbols are unapproachable. They find the vertical language so strange that even if Christianity is made as understandable as possible—by removing unnecessary stumbling blocks of absurdity and primitivism—they still have great difficulty. Their barrier to understanding the dimension of the unconditional (the ultimate, or infinite), as I have observed, is their thoroughly objectifying attitude. In order to define anything, you must objectify it—make it finite. *Definere* (the Latin root) means circumscribing a finite reality. Therefore all problems of something unconditional, ultimate, or infinite—not in the mathematical but the qualitative sense—are strange to the typical modern person. For these matters cannot be construed in terms of finitude or definition.

Then another element comes into the picture. Typically modern thinking, which makes everything in the world (including humans) into mere

objects, excludes a relation to reality that under-
lies all Christian thinking: the love relationship.
This is true in theology and in ethics. It embraces
the *eros* relationship of the philosopher, the *philia*
relationship among humans, and the *agape* relationship of seeing in everything a manifestation of the
divine ground of being and accepting it as such.
All this is strange to those who live only in the
controlling horizontal and have lost the vertical.
What is left of *eros*—and often it is much in these
persons—has been pushed into the merely emotional realm. Their knowledge, on the other hand,
is completely unemotional. But there are dimen-
sions of reality where we must participate in order to know. And participation in order to know
demands participation of the whole person.

Christianity defends itself, but in doing so it unconsciously moves on the same level against which
it would defend itself—the level of mere objectification. It turns the symbolic stories of biblical
literature into objectified events. It does what it
should fight against. This makes the situation extremely difficult. In centuries in which this objectification had not yet taken place, or not yet
grasped most people, myth, legend, and history
were mixed. There was no real difference between
them, and a miracle story was not more difficult
to accept than a so-called historical story. But in
the moment that the modern mind realized the
difference of history, legend, and myth—and efforts were made to defend the biblical stories as
objectively demonstrable—the Christian case was

lost. The defenders had surrendered their defensive power. They could not help, and the symbols of the vertical line were not saved but distorted. This is one of the many reasons for the irrelevance of the Christian message.

There is another point: authority against autonomy. When we hear these words, there are two misunderstandings. Many people may reply to everything I have said: "But you didn't refer to the authority of the Word of God." Or, "You didn't refer to the authority of the Catholic tradition." In saying so they understand this authority to relate to verifiable facts as scientists state them. But in this sense the Word of God and the church have no authority. No historical, or physical or psychological statement is ever guaranteed by Bible or church. Such statements belong to the realm of finite relations and therefore are open to scientific inquiry. But there is also an opposite misunderstanding of autonomy or freedom of thought. Deciding about ultimate principles autonomously does not mean willfulness. Although the Greek roots *auto* (self) and *nomos* (law) may seem to indicate this, what autonomy really means is following obediently and humbly the structures of reality as the mind can take them. We rightly speak of the Word of God when we mean something ecstatic which we may experience in human words of all kinds, not just between two covers of a book. In every human interrelation the Word of God can become actual. It is a breaking in out of another dimension. But it is not telling us anything about physics, biology, psychology, or history. When Christianity speaks of autonomy it means obedience. Or better, it means being grasped by the Divine Spirit and then deciding in freedom. For where the Divine Spirit grasps a human it does not suppress, but liberates each one to full freedom.

What about the attack of "relativism" against all contents of belief and ethics? There is no relativism with respect to the experience of the Unconditional in oneself. But there is the relativity of all history with respect to the religious symbols and the ethical commands. *They* are not unconditional. They are historically conditioned and changing. They all stand under the one unconditional criterion: *agape,* the Christian word for love. This is not a law, but is the negation of every law. It is in itself unconditional because nothing can transcend love and nothing less than love is sufficient. But what love is in the concrete moment is open to the creative understanding of the situation and does not have the character of a law we can define and obey.

There is a further interesting point I want to mention because it is so characteristic today of our Western situation. This is the alliance of the modern scientific mind with the Asiatic mystical mind. The invasion of Buddhist propaganda into the West, not only in unserious but in very serious forms, reflects the irrelevance of Christianity we have been considering. But what is the reason for it? Why are so many people, in the educated groups especially, drawn toward Buddhist, especially Zen, solutions? I shall offer two possible reasons. One

might be what I have been describing: that the
Christian symbols have been objectified by their
defenders and, by this very fact, have lost their
meaning and power. They have come to be understood literally, as events in time and space, taught
on biblical authority. This, as referring to the ultimate dimension, the modern mind cannot accept.
So moderns turn to a religion in which such objectification is not possible. The mystical mind transcends every objectification in religion as well as
in culture.[4] So it is felt that here perhaps Asia may
help us. But there might be an additional reason.
If true it would be of deepest significance. (I do
not know whether it is true, but will state it for
consideration.) What Zen Buddhism calls the
"formless self," the self beyond subject and object,
it regards as the extinction of definite individuality in the highest experience of enlightenment.
Now this might appeal to the modern Western
mind which, in our technical mass society, has lost
its own affirmation of the significance of the individual. I leave it to my readers to ask yourselves
whether a hidden desire might be in you to get
rid of your responsibility for yourselves by tran-
scending individuality.

I shall close this chapter by pointing to something I regard as a profound reaction against the
modern mind as I have been describing it. The
name for it is the much abused and misunderstood
term "existentialism." It is the "way around" which
(as often before) history, or, if you will, divine
providence, has given to make Christianity relevant

again. Existentialism does this by showing the emptiness of the merely horizontal line. The sense of this emptiness has grown, from Pascal, to whom I referred above, to the great conceptualizers of existentialism in the nineteenth century, to the large-scale acceptance of the reaction in the twentieth century.[5] Existentialism is a diagnosis of the situation of the modern personality, of the negativity of a world determined only by the horizontal line, by calculating reason and objectifying control. It shows there is something else: namely our finitude, anxiety, guilt, loneliness, and meaninglessness. Existentialist literature and art—and also philosophical conceptualization—have shown through this the human reality out of which the question came, again and again in all ages, to which the Christian symbols were once understood as answers.

The way history has taken was always first to reveal the question, or have humanity itself ask it, and then point here and there to different answers: some of them Christian, some not. So it seems to me we may consider this arising of existentialist interpretation as the divine providential way to make it at least possible again to understand the Christian symbols as answers to actual questions. If this were done, then the Christian symbols would again become *possible* answers to be rejected or accepted. This would already be a new relevance.

Every minister and religious teacher should go through the phase of diving into the depths of the question which the human being is. If this is impossible in personal experience, then certainly it should be done in empathetic understanding. If it is impossible in all realms of existentialist diagnosis, at least it should be done in some of them. Especially important is understanding the structure of the existing human being as an individual personality. For what is relevant to anyone is what answers the question which "I myself" am.

3

The Revolt against the Modern Mind: The Relevance of the Christian Message in Spite of Its Irrelevance

The previous chapter combined a tremendous amount of material in trying to analyze what in the present situation is the cause for the irrelevance of the Christian message described in the first chapter. This combining of many elements in picturing the cause of the irrelevance of the Christian message provides a means for understanding the present situation in which we all are, if not consciously, then certainly unconsciously. Now I want to go back to the final point in the last chapter when I spoke about the revolt against the fundamental characteristics of the modern mind, coming from what is usually called, mostly with a too narrow concept, the existentialist movement. I characterized this movement as the attempt to describe the human situation in its existential predicament, our condition here and now, and not only humanity's essential, created, true, good, dynamic, progressive nature.

This is the point where I want to connect this concluding chapter with the whole analysis I have been giving of the present situation of humanity and its world. Existentialism has its greatness as a revolt. It is a revolt which started as early as the modern mind. Already in the seventeenth century Pascal combined both the essentialist and the existentialist elements in his own person, foreshadowing one of the deepest conflicts produced by the development of the modern mind. On the one hand, there is the attitude of controlling nature and society through the power of calculating reason, the attitude of going ahead and ahead and ahead in the horizontal dimension of human life. I call it somewhere "forwardism"—always forward and never knowing for what, only forward. And on the other hand, there is the real human being who is finite, who experiences the anxiety of finitude, who is guilty even if not feeling guilty of anything specific. Real human beings are guilty of not being what they ought to be and could be. They do not know the meaning of their life. They ask passionately and sometimes cynically the question of the meaning of life. Now, this split in modern humanity is the end of a long development. When I described this development, I mentioned the one side of the split called the human predicament or existentialist analysis. These phrases express the same awareness. I illustrated its beginning in a man like Pascal, and showed it culminating in human life today. But between this beginning and ending lie the great revolutionaries of the nineteenth century, people in philosophy like Schelling, in theology like Kierkegaard, in politics and social analysis like Marx, in the philosophy of life like Nietzsche. All these men foreshadowed what in our century became the predominant style of writing, thinking, painting, and all the other expressions of the human spirit. But when we ask the question about the relevancy of the Christian message in spite of its irrelevancy, it is not enough to point to the existentialist revolt. Although it became victorious in all great cultural expressions in the middle of the twentieth century, existentialism is not enough. The analysis of the human predicament does not answer the question of the meaning of human existence. The great existentialists since Pascal up to today have not given answers as existentialists. The existentialist analysis of the world situation determines the direction and the form of the answer. But in all of the existentialists the answer came from somewhere else, not from the analysis, not from the human predicament, but from the world of essences. That means from traditions, philosophies, literature, theology, in which the true nature of humanity is seen and described. It could not be otherwise because analysis of the gap between what we essentially are and what we in reality are does not communicate an answer. The answer comes from elsewhere.

In an essay on existentialism one could go into its major representatives and show which of the great Western traditions are behind the answers of each one. But this is not our problem here. Our problem is Christianity. Is Christianity able to give answers to the questions raised by the existentialist analysis of the human predicament in time and space? Is Christianity able to answer on the basis of what it essentially is, in spite of all its distortions in time and space? Is it able to give answer both to the typically modern mind and to the existentialist revolt against the modern mind?

I answer yes. It can. But in order to give the foundation for this answer, I must ask you to follow again, as in the previous chapters, difficult roads of thought. There will have to be abbreviations of matters that in themselves would demand several lectures, whereas here they will get only several words. I will first try to show those characteristics of Christianity which may be able to answer the questions arising both from the problem of the modern mind and from those who have given the analysis called existentialist.

Let me first state a factor in Christianity which can in general make it relevant today. This is an event *which has happened,* an event which consists of two parts: the fact of a personal life, and the reception of this life by a group called disciples or followers. This is the event on which everything else is dependent. I repeat, the event has two sides: the factual side and the receiving side; and both are necessary. Christ, in strict theological terms, would not be the Christ without the church, that is, the community that received him. And the church could not be the church without the Christ on whom the church is based. Now this means that Christianity is not based on an idea or a set of symbols. They are there. They are used. But the church is based on something that has happened in time and space—the appearance of a man who is called Jesus, who was received by the disciples as the expected Christ. With this event underlying Christianity, it was far superior to the high religious movements with which it had to compete. Whatever the interpretation might be, one could always go back to the image of this event given in the biblical literature, and to the reality shining through this image. We do not know how much comes from the side of the fact and how much from the side of the reception. For the religious purpose we do not need to know. For the historiographical understanding of the development of the biblical writings and the early church, it is very important to know. This element of event guarantees something which transcends all competing religions without such a foundation. It has a uniqueness which every historical event has—incomparable and inexhaustible. This is the background of the essential relevance of Christianity, the relevance of an event in the whole of human events with universal human significance.

This event was received in the church traditions, which were combined in the process leading, four hundred years later, to the biblical canon. Afterwards they went on developing from century to century. As this happened the churches not only preserved and explained the event. They also concealed and distorted it. Again and again they made it ununderstandable, unreceivable and irrelevant.

I spoke previously of the fight of the great theologians through the whole of church history to make the event relevant again in their time. One could say they represent the Kingdom of God and also that they conceal and distort the Kingdom of God. I call this the paradox of the churches, and whoever does not understand this paradox does not understand what church is. The churches represent the Spiritual Community which is not only actual in them, but which is actual all over the world in what I have sometimes called the "latent church." This is the church which has not yet come to the surface but is present in the religions and cultures of humankind everywhere. The churches represent this Spiritual Community which is hidden and manifest at the same time. But also they betray continuously this community, for instance by preventing the criticism against themselves which comes from the latent church, the underground Spiritual Community all over the world that is found also in humanism and in all the other forms of secular existence.

When I look at the actual churches, I often am horrified by the tremendous depths of this paradox: to represent the Kingdom of God or, in other words, the Spiritual Community, and at the same time to betray it, conceal it, and distort it. But when the distortion hits me so deeply I incline to turn away from the churches, then suddenly in a little service in a small church or in an act of love inspired by biblical symbols, by the image of Jesus, something breaks through all the weakness, banality, and corruption of actual church life. This has happened probably to all of us again and again. It is what made it possible for this distorted representation of the Spiritual Community to go on from generation to generation. The decisive thing in all this is that the church remains aware of the paradox of its existence.

The New Testament church was still aware of it. In the records we have reports of the fight of Jesus with the apostles about the meaning of his mission and his death. Only through his death can he be the Messiah.[1] This is the basic paradox of Christianity over against the unparadoxical, religiously primitive attitude of the disciples. Most churches are followers of the disciples in the fight of Jesus against them. This appears again and again in the history of the church in the glorification of the forms which embody the ultimate meaning of the event. The embodiment itself was glorified rather than what was embodied. And this is still the case. But there were again and again attacks on the churches because they forgot their own paradox and made themselves untouchable, unconditionally right and good. The greatest attack, upon many fundamentals which had developed in church history, was made by the Protestant Reformation. For this reason I like to call the principle of this attack the "Protestant Principle."[2] It is the principle in which the church in its essence, or true being, protests against the church in its existence. From this it follows there must always be two things in church life: the duality of tradition and reformation. If either disappears completely, then Christianity is gone; there is no chance that a stiffened, lifeless Christianity can become relevant again.

The decisive implication of this paradox of the

churches is the possibility to liberate Christianity from any cultural fixation and open it for new embodiments in other worlds and other periods. I refer to differences of culture, nations, and times, and beyond these to something even more fundamental: the essential differences about the meaning of human existence which underlie religions and cultures. Christianity, as I said earlier, expresses humanity's self-interpretation in the vertical line—the line above to the unconditional. But Christianity is able to take into itself the horizontal line—in which we live today almost exclusively—without losing the vertical line. Christianity is even able to take into itself the circular line of classical Greece and thus affirm humanism's ideal of fulfilling all human potentialities. Christianity is able to embrace both the period where the world was a closed sphere and our period of "forwardism"—the going ahead and ahead which has become decisive for all of us. For in Christianity the vertical is not something immovable but is a dynamic power open for many realities. Therefore Christianity is also able to take the foreign religions into itself—under one condition. That is the same condition for which Jesus fought against his disciples: namely, the condition that everything finite has to sacrifice itself to that which is infinite in order to become a bearer of the infinite. To avoid this sacrifice is the demonic distortion of religion. All religions, including Christianity, are demonically distorted because they elevate their finite reality to the ultimate. It is true that they stand for the ultimate. I call them representatives of the Kingdom of God or of the Spiritual Community. But if they do more than stand for the ultimate—if they divinize themselves—then they become demonic. Wherever in history the demonic appears, in religion and outside of religion, we see the elevation of something finite to infinite validity.

We must now look at a phenomenon which is a key to the whole history of religion: the fight of religion against religion. There are two reasons for this fight. The first is the demonization of religion, as just considered. All great leaders of religious reform and new birth fight against earlier demonic forms of religion. In India as well as Israel, in Christianity as well as Buddhism, religion claims to represent the conditional, the absolute. But in the moment in which religion makes itself absolute, it is an expression of the demonic, the destructive distortion of the holy. The second reason for the fight of religion against religion is that the divine according to its very essence is present in the secular world. This is clear in many expressions of the thought and life of the Old and New Testaments as well as the church. Accordingly, the division between the secular sphere and the religious sphere expresses the basic evil in humanity's predicament. The ultimate ideal, the form in which humanity would realize its essential truth, is the ideal of non-religion and non-secular, the identity of workday and Sunday, the manifestation of the divine in everything in which we live.

Now the fight of religion against religion is obvious in Christianity when it judges all types of religion, primarily the two types which were present in the period of early Christianity, the Jews and the Greeks. "Greeks" is the cultural name at that time for a type of humanism, but one which is based on pagan religions and forms of faith. Christianity's judgment against Jews and pagans—read the first chapters of the Letter to the Romans—was thus not a fight against irreligion so much as against religion. Certainly Paul was not irreligious; neither was Jesus. But Paul fights because of his insight that "nothing matters," as he puts it, "neither circumcision [which means Judaism] nor uncircumcision [which means paganism] but only a new reality," which is the event of the Christ.[3] This is not restricted to Christianity, although in Christianity it has received perhaps its most paradoxical character. The relevance of Christianity is asserted by its self-negation. Without this continuous self-negation, Christianity is not true Christianity and is not relevant.[4]

But we must go a step beyond this, because self-negation alone is not saving power. It is only saving if it is based on something positive, on the highest form of self-affirmation. This positivity in Christianity, which alone makes its self-negation so great, is the event of which I spoke, the appearance of Jesus who was called the Christ, as a new reality in history. He is the new reality of humanity or the "new being," as I like to call it: the new being which in its essence is infinitely relevant for all existence. This is the reality of which we can speak which is relevant. It is relevant in its very nature, whatever a period of history will do with it—how it can receive it, or how it is blocked against receiving it. The Pauline term for this reality is "new creature" or "new creation." I call it the "new being" for particular reasons not to discuss now.[5] What this new being does is overcome the conflict between essential being and distorted existence: between the created goodness of being and its disruptions as shown in the human predicament. In the image of Christ we find the traits of this new power. What we see is the astonishing fact—the paradoxical fact—that in the midst of human existence we find an image of essential humanity. It is not an "ideal," something merely hoped for or prophetically announced, as in the Old Testament (and, in fact, in the whole history of religion). Here it is seen as a *reality* which radiates through Jesus' image, as that was remembered by the disciples when they received it.

What is this new reality or new being that conquers the split between humanity's essential goodness and its existential distortion? First there is the anti-demonic self-sacrifice. This is the decisive point of my whole answer about the relevance of Christianity. All the temptations of Jesus, not only in the desert but throughout the New Testament story, are demonic temptations to make himself in his finitude absolute without the self-sacrificial death. I say the greatness and relevance of Christianity root in the fact that this image, as we have it in the Bible and tradition, is the end of every religious as well as every political absolutism. The powers of religion and the powers of politics brought him to the cross. On this basis we have the first trait of the new reality in the picture of the Christ and its inexhaustible power.[6]

What does this mean for the individual? New being means for all of us one unheard-of thing—one almost impossible thing, if we are serious: namely, self-acceptance. You may answer, "Nothing is easier. We all accept ourselves, love ourselves, and like to stay with ourselves as long as possible on this earth." So why make this the fundamental point of the new being? This self-acceptance is partly our natural self-affirmation, and it is partly a continuous repression of disgust with ourselves. I never have met a serious human being who did not tell me the story of his or her self-disgust, which makes right self-love impossible. If this self-disgust is there and is felt—if the voice is heard which says "You are not what you essentially are, not your image (*eidos*) in God's mind, symbolically speaking, but a distortion of that"—then self-acceptance becomes the deepest and most difficult question.[7]

Here we have two widespread positions. The one is the position of the law which condemns. It runs through all the history of religion and Christianity, from the Old Testament in its early periods to the Pharisees in the last period, to the Puritans in our culture and the evangelical and revival movements. Everywhere we have the law which condemns—or worse, which brings people to a self-affirmation on the basis of the goodness they see in themselves. This is the one way. The other way is that of the mystics in all religions, the basically Asiatic way—namely a resignation which negates the self as such, and thus every self and every life ultimately.

Against both positions, I believe it is the unique greatness of Christianity that it shows the positivity of life in the principle which has had many names in Christian history but which I like to call "the acceptance of the unacceptable," namely, the acceptance of *us.* You can call it divine grace, or justification by grace through faith, or you can give it other names. Here I do not use the old words, but try to find another expression. From psychoanalysis I have learned that the unacceptable must first be accepted and only then can be transformed. And so I say it is the greatness of Christianity that it shows the positivity of life over against the condemning or self-justifying law *and* over against the profound resignation of life in much of the Eastern world.

Of course this presupposes that there is a power of "grace"—again a word which is terribly troubling because of its innumerable wrong or even nonsensical connotations. But there is a principle or a reality in life itself which breaks through in moments of self-disgust and self-condemnation and which can affirm that one is accepted, although one knows how unacceptable one is. Our striving is never finished. Perfection, the return to what we essentially are on a higher level, is never reached. And so we look for what Goethe, at the

55

end of the second part of Faust, calls "the grace from above, which must participate in us."[8] This grace is not a divine emergency action which sometimes breaks into our predicament, but is the actual paradox in which we live. It is always present and sometimes, when we are open because of our self-disgust, it may grasp us and give us the experience of a new life or a new being.

For this new reality has saving power. "Saving" originally means healing. Salvation means the process or the result of healing, healing in every direction. Therefore there are the many healing stories in the New Testament. They are not interesting as so-called "miracles,"[9] but as the existence of a power of healing in the world—be it from a powerful person, be it by medical practice, be it by the inner power of the sick themselves, who may have healing powers which come to the surface. All these ways are possible. As Christians, we see in Jesus the image of a human being in whom grace was present without limit, as in the story of the twelve-year-old Jesus in the temple.[10] But grace can happen otherwise, in many ways. It can happen in the simplest acts of life: what you do in your household, or in your factory, or your office or studio, or outside in nature, or in love relations of all kinds. It does not need religion. God does not make grace dependent on the existence of religion. God is greater than the religion in which God is manifest. If we understand this and see it is indicated not only in many words of Jesus and Paul but in the very fact of the Cross, then we have some understanding why it might be possible to make Christianity relevant again.

A question that has plagued me for many years is whether Christianity can conquer meaninglessness—the feeling of emptiness, cynicism, of radical doubt—all these deepest forms of negativity as they appear in the existentialist literature and art of the twentieth century. I believe it is possible, but would not prophesy it will happen easily. It is possible for two reasons. First, in the feeling of meaninglessness there is always an element of hostility against the world, not just against particular persons but life itself. And the reconciliation of which Paul speaks is a reconciliation with the ground of our being: thus with our world, with life universally, and with ourselves. Since Christianity has in itself this threefold reconciliation, it has one step towards overcoming, along with hostility, also the feeling of meaninglessness.

But there is a second step, and this is *agape*. I hesitate to use the word "love," because today our impoverished language about spiritual things has only this one word for what the Greeks were wise enough to have four. One was *epithymia*, in Latin *libido*, the hunger and thirst for what we need and must strive. The second was *philia*, friendship, the person-to-person relationship in which we choose those whom we love. The third Greek word was *eros*, present in those scientists whose work aspires for the whole of physical reality and through it the ultimate, but also present in the arts and literature as they aim for the good, true, and beautiful. Then, higher than these three, purifying and elevating them, there is the fourth form of love. This is *agape,* the love which accepts the unacceptable, the one we cannot like, which loves the enemy for whom we cannot have sympathy. That is the way God loves us, according to the New Testament, and Christianity has this experience of love.

I have also found love in all its forms elsewhere. In Japan, *agape* is not expressed as in Christianity. It is much more compassion. But, with Japanese Buddhists, you see what this compassion can do and are ashamed of your Christian *agape*—not because of the *agape* but because of yourself.

So there is *agape* in the compassion of the Japanese. But the pure, clear principle of acceptance of the unacceptable—and therefore of reconciliation and healing in the ultimate sense—is nowhere expressed as radically and fully as in Christianity.

Just today, from an African attending the lectures, I learned how many elements of *agape* are present in the tribal traditions of Africa, creating a relevant approach for the Christian preaching of *agape.*

Where there is reconciliation and *agape* there is no meaninglessness anymore. There is rather the experience of eternal life here and now. There is no eternal life which is not before *and* present *and* after—and that means beyond every mode of time. Eternal is not temporal, and eternal life is not life in the hereafter. Eternal life is life now, and before our being in time and space, and after our being in time and space. But these words "before" and "after" lose their meaning. They are symbolic pointers to the fact that eternity is beyond the temporal process. When we "return to eternity" we do not return. We do not continue our existence in time and space—not even on heavenly meadows—but we are reunited with the eternal ground from which we came and to which we go.

Let me ask again: how can Christianity be relevant under these conditions? I believe the preceding description has largely answered this question. But let us go a little further into the answer.

Without expression or manifestation everything remains merely potential and does not become actual. Thus, everything I have said about Christianity must have a manifestation to be real. I said "No Christ without the church," which means Jesus could not become manifest as the bearer of the new being without those who receive him as such. The expression of this reception is manifold. It is there in the life of the church, in its symbols of thought and action.

But again there is a gap between essential reality and expression. As artists know, every expression is something daring that might not express but only conceal. So it is with us. On the basis of insights into our situation, we try to express the Christian event, the new reality. But our expression perhaps conceals more than it manifests this reality. This risk the church must take! The minister who simply preaches in traditional ways, without risking error and controversy, should not have become a minister. Ministry means service, and he or she does not serve—does not heal, but rather prevents healing.

We considered the horizontal dimension—going ahead and ahead. Although able to take the horizontal and the circular into itself, Christianity is based on the vertical dimension. But what is this vertical dimension? When we try to explain it to people today, let us not start with the "question of God." For people of our objectified world take "God" as an object whose existence or nonexistence is debated like that of another galaxy. This denies the divinity of the divine. Let us start instead with what we have, what we really are—our ultimate concern, which is implied in everything positive and negative in our life. Let us start here, not because it is a clever method, but because it is our most personal experience. I mean the power and universality of the divine, which transcends everything we can *say* about the divine. Let us avoid objectifying statements about the holy. Let us avoid giving it names, even the traditional ones of theology. When we do give it names—as we must in speaking of it, or even in silent prayer—then let us always have a yes and a no in our statements. It is remarkable how the biblical language, especially the Old Testament, presents a very concrete God whom it seems everyone could make into an object alongside other objects. But try it. This God will evade you. You never can fix this God. Hence the prohibition to name God, since a name is something you can grasp, something which tries to "define" or make finite. This is the greatness of the biblical language. It avoids objectifying. In all great religious experiences, the divine appears and disappears—a thing Calvin still knew. For this we have the word "epiphany," which means the appearing of an ungraspable divine power—being there and not being there. This "yes *and* no" is the foundation of all speaking about the divine. Thus may the vertical line of the divine enter the horizontal dynamics of human history.

The early church had to resist the Roman Empire. In terrible struggles and through martyrdom Christianity prevailed. Today *we* have to resist the meaningless "forwardism" determining our inner and outer existence. Most of us can offer this resistance only as victims of the structures of our time: the structures of objectification in the horizontal dynamics of controlling knowledge. I confess this is true of me. We can resist only as victims. But the scars received in our lives may be the basis for a sensitive speaking. More than this I could not say of myself, and I believe few of you could say more about your own situation. Now this may lead to rediscovery of the depth dimension, the vertical depth in everything encountered. But even then we will have to keep on resisting—against control by others, against "management" of persons, against all abuse of men and women. This certainly includes the abuse of forcing them into their own salvation, as discussed in the previous chapter. Nature

Likewise must we resist abusing nature as a mere "thing" to be controlled. If we had a different feeling toward nature, we would have a different feeling for the wholeness and holiness of life. *Not* having this contributes to our loss of everything sacramental—because if the whole universe is not seen sacramentally, the partial sacraments die off. And in all *cultural* creations too we must show the presence of the holy. We need an understanding of culture not only measured by productivity but in terms of the ultimate meaning that shines through—through the most seemingly atheistic novels and the most radically anti-human visual art of our time. This ultimate meaning shines as well through the different political experiments all over the world, shines through social systems, even through one of the worst forms of objectifying persons—modern advertising. In their unholiness all these things nevertheless have a point that, however small, is inexpressibly strong: the divine ground that shines through every creative human act.

Now what is the church in all this? With this I will conclude. The church is several things. She is a treasure chest which is often closed, which we must open again and again. She is a counterbalance against the secular indifference to which our human predicament makes us prone. She is a representative of the depth and height of the vertical line. In principle, prayer and contemplation should not be special acts. But sometimes we need to flee into them from the restlessness of the horizontal line. Yet they never should be made into absolutes, as the church should never be made absolute. Hear this one important warning! Never consider the secular realm Godless just because it it does not speak of God. To speak of a realm of divine creation and providence as Godless *is* Godless. It denies God's power over the world. It would force God to confine Godself to religion and church.

Thus I come to the end of what I would say. I have asked and do ask all of you who are responsible for the church and Christianity—ministers, laity, those on the boundary, even those outside—to *fight an uphill battle!* In this battle the decision will be made whether Christianity's essential and universal relevance will again become an actual relevance for our period of history.

Notes

1. The Avowed Irrelevance of Christian Preaching to the Contemporary World

1. The precise title is *On Religion: Speeches to the Cultured among Its Despisers* (Berlin, 1799).

2. Before World War I, teaching a confirmation class, Tillich sensed the word "faith" had become meaningless. In 1912 he organized "reason evenings" for laity, to engage the doubts of the estranged. Cf. W. and M. Pauck, *Paul Tillich: His Life and Thought* (New York: Harper, 1976), 37.

3. The Second Vatican Council, convened by Pope John XXIII, was under way as Tillich spoke.

4. Winter's book with this title was published by Doubleday in 1961.

5. Matthew 5:3.

6. Tillich's classic explanation of this difference is given in his *Dynamics of Faith* (New York: Harper Torchbook, 1957).

7. In addition to his own extensive counseling, Tillich was indebted here to H. Richard Niebuhr's *The Purpose of the Church and Its Ministry* (New York: Harper, 1956).

8. Cf. 2 Corinthians 12:10. The RSV reads "when I am weak . . ."

9. Tillich is referring here to his experience in Germany before his emigration in 1933.

2. The Nature of Present-Day Thought: Its Strangeness to Traditional Christianity

1. During the 1950s and 1960s, B. F. Skinner was generally viewed as the leading theoretician of psychological behaviorism. He had published *Walden Two,* which envisages a utopia, in 1961.

2. In this and the following sentence one may assume Tillich today would have used "Native American" rather than "red Indian." Further, his metaphor in this sentence seems misleadingly inspired by the romanticized "Wild West" imaged in his childhood Germany by the novelist Karl May. "Nature preserve" would serve Tillich better, though that would not fit the following sentence.

3. In the twentieth century some theologians, notably Barth and Bonhoeffer, have rejected the categorization of essential Christianity as a religion. Tillich appears to refer to this possible stance in mentioning Christianity as an irreligion.

4. What Tillich means here is most fully spelled out by him in his pioneering 1957 dialogue at Harvard with Zen Master Hisamatsu Shin-ichi. The text is available in Tillich, *The Encounter of Religions and Quasi-Religions,* ed. Terry Thomas (Lewiston, N.Y.: Edwin Mellen, 1990), 75–170.

5. The nineteenth-century figures Tillich has pre-eminently in mind are Schelling, Kierkegaard, and Nietzsche, though he also saw Marx and Freud as pivotal contributors to the wider existentialist impact. Twentieth-century acceptance of existentialism, which was *more* widespread on the European continent than in America, was frequently illustrated by him in art and literature. Its main philosophical expositors were Heidegger, Jaspers, and Sartre.

3. The Revolt against the Modern Mind: The Relevance of the Christian Message in Spite of Its Irrelevance

1. Tillich offers basic explication of this salient thesis in *Systematic Theology* (Chicago: University of Chicago Press, 1951, 1957), vol. I, 135–36, and vol. II, 123–24.

2. Note that the Protestant Principle, one of Tillich's basic themes, is not limited by him to historic Protestantism. It is exemplified wherever pretensions of the finite to be more than finite are brought under the judgment of the Unconditional.

3. Tillich spells out this thought in his sermon "The New Being," available in *The New Being* (New York: Scribner's, 1955), 15–24. The text is Galatians 6:15.

4. An extension, of course, of the necessity of Christ's Cross, as stated above.

5. An extended discussion is offered by Tillich in *Systematic Theology* (cited above), vol. II, 118 ff.

6. A different ordering of the traits of the "new reality in Christ" is used by Tillich in the *Systematic Theology*. E.g., vol. II, p. 138, states that the new reality shines through Jesus' picture "in a threefold color . . . first and decisively as the undisrupted unity of the center of his being with God; second, as the serenity and majesty of him who preserves this unity against all the attacks coming from estranged existence; and, third, as the self-surrendering love which represents and actualizes the divine love in taking the existential self-destruction upon himself." This variation of order is feasible in that systematically all traits of the Christ imply each other, while the change in the Earl Lectures does indicate, at this phase of Tillich's thought, a prioritizing of the Cross that is even higher than at some ear-

lier phases. However, already in *Systematic Theology,* vol. I, p. 133, the Cross is the very first thing alluded to in the criterion of anyone being the Christ ("negating oneself without losing oneself"). Notice at the same time the immediately conjoined reference to the resurrection.

7. Tillich's most eloquent exposition regarding acceptance was widely felt to be his sermon "You Are Accepted," available in *The Shaking of the Foundations* (New York: Scribner's, 1948), 153–63.

8. The text of *Faust* has "the love from above."

9. In Tillich's native German there are two words for miracle. Behind the disavowal of "miracle" here we should hear "*Mirakel,*" which connotes intervention in the natural order. The other German word, "*Wunder,*" connotes a manifestation of the divine. Tillich affirmed miracle in this sense as integral to revelation.

10. In the Luther Bible, on which Tillich cut his scriptural teeth, the last verse of the temple story (Luke 2:52) has Jesus growing in "grace" where English versions have "favor."

Index

Index

Index

interest, 21
Isaac, 29
Islam, xviii
Israel, 51

Jacob, 29
Jaspers, Karl, xv, xvi, 66
Jesus: grace of, 56; as life of
    the church, 59; sentimen-
    talization of, 15–16;
    temptations of, 53–54.
    See also Christ
Jesus seminar, xxii
John XXIII, 65
Judaism, xviii, 52

Kaehler, Martin, xx
Kant, Immanuel, 7
kerygmatic theology, x
Kierkegaard, Soren, 8, 44, 66
Kingdom of God, xiv, 35,
    47–48, 51
knowledge, technical
    control of, xv–xvi, xxv

labor movement, 20
language, irrelevance of, 14–
    16
latent church, 48
Law: condemnation of, 54–
    55; in preaching, 16–17
Leonardo da Vinci, 29
Letter to the Romans, 52
liberation theology, xii

libido, 57
love (*agape*), xxiii–xiv, 36, 38,
    57–59
Luther, Martin, xxiii, 5, 8, 9

Marburg, Germany, 7
Marx, Karl, 32, 44, 66
May, Karl, 66
McLuhan, Marshall, xviii
meaninglessness, 57–59
mediation, theology of, 8–9,
    23
message-centered theology, x
method of correlation, x–xii
ministers, personalities of, 19–
    20
miracles, 68
modern mind, 23–41; revolt
    against, 43–63
mysticism, 6, 38–39, 55

nature, control of, 24–25, 61–
    62
Nazis, xii
new beginnings, 9–10, 26
New Being in Jesus as the
    Christ, xi, xxii–xxiii, 52–
    54
New York School for Social
    Research, xii
Niebuhr, H. Richard, xxiv,
    xxvii, 65
Nietzsche, Friedrich, 32–33,
    44, 66

72

Index